The My Heart Blues

The My Heart Blues

by Lamont Arrington

ISBN: 978-1-968226-09-1

Grand River Poetry Press
Grand Rapids, Michigan

Thank you Jeffrey Bean and Robert Fanning for your guidance on my journey through graduate school at Central Michigan University as I wrote this book. Thank you Jericho Brown for the duplex. Thank you Nick West for the many open mics where I read and strengthened these poems. Thank you Jasmyn for reintroducing me to my heart. Without you this work would not be possible. Thank you.

This book is for her.

Table of Contents

II The Bad

III The Dark

IV The Ugly

I The Good

You Make Me Feel I Can Speak

The world swallows my mind. Now I can't think.
I look you in the eyes and see trees burn.

  I look in the trees and see you burning.
  Everything I love remains on fire.

I love every fire. Things remain
fleeting. I want what won't turn into ash.

  What I want is fleet. I turn into ash.
  I need someone to know I'm still here.

Here, someone needs me. I know I'm still
a broken soldier, an absent brother,

  a broken pencil, and absent money.
  All I have left is what sparks from my heart.

I spark my heart with all that I have left.
Swallow my mind. I think the world of you.

Don't Hide From Me

We know what it means
for us to burn like this.
We feel the sun's warmth
cradled in each other's gravity.
We give up our names,
we give up our hearts,
we become pieces
of a whole puzzle.
We shape ourselves
from dirt and leaves.
Our garden blooms
lavender, blueberries,
matcha, and chai.
We never go hungry
full of each moment.
Strangers envy us
glowing in darkness.
We only see light –
there's no end to what
echoes between us.
There's so much
we can share it.
We are refreshed.
Times have changed,
forever is too few years
to discover what's left.
Inch by inch we kiss
and tomorrow arrives.

There’s no remedy
for this affliction, no magic,
no godly touch to mend
what's stolen our days.
Our bodies shake for minutes
hugging goodbye. Our minds
never leave. We sleep
connected by breath,
lit by what wakes us.

I Hated My Life Without Her

A chunk of me was lost when I was young.
In my dirt filled heart I grew over it.

Over my heart I grew a tree in dirt.
It's the only thing I love. Here, I'm free

from the wind chasing me. Here, I'm in love.
I live my life tending to the tree eating me.

Life tends me. I live eating tree branches,
no one has told me I can taste the fruit.

The fruit has told me no one can taste it.
I believe the words that spring from my heart.

In spring, I believe the words my heart says
when I plant her in my dirt. Her heart blooms.

Her heart is like mine. In her dirt I bloom
chunks of me, all I lost when I was young.

We Flourished When My Heart Let You In

You built my heart a leafy home to rest
of flowers grown from the palms of your hands.

> You grew flowers from your palms that smell of ink,
> they leave black butterflies in my heart's dreams.

My heart dreams of black butterflies leaving
pink kisses on each sprout in its garden.

> In the garden each sprout has a pink kiss,
> they're still there when my heart wakes from its sleep.

It wakes from its sleep while you're still there,
sees you glowing in the dark with the sprouts

> glowing in the dark, sees you with the sprouts
> and feels the world gave it a clear answer.

The world is clear when I feel you answer
my heart. It loves its leafy home the best.

My Mother Has Interrogated Me My Entire Life

I don’t know how to tell you the whole truth.
I say it in pieces. Chop it to bits.

When I chop it up I fall to pieces
trying to help you follow what I mean.

What I mean is I don’t follow your try
at conversation. No questions? No shouts?

I shout questions during conversation,
I want to know what's hidden in your heart.

When I know what's hidden I see your heart
beating out your chest. It gets tense as hell.

It gets so tense I feel like beating you
just to bring some sense into the chaos.

I bring chaos and turn it into sense,
it’s how I know you told me the whole truth.

Speechless

It’s language we speak with just our tongues,
words I can’t say to anyone but you.

> Anyone but you can say words to me –
> in wool blankets I understand our truth.

The truth in wool blankets is understood
sleeping on a couch regretting answers.

> I regret answering you, I can’t sleep,
> shouldn’t have brought fire to your warm bed.

Your bed is warm because of my fire,
won’t you let me take a piece for myself?

> I give pieces of myself you won’t take,
> test the limits of how bright we can be.

There’s a limit to how bright we can be
with just our tongues. We need new language.

My Heart Shares The Garden With You

My heart won't let me near it since you came
to tend the garden. It closes the door.

    It tends to close the door to the garden.
    It's got nothing to do with you and me.

You do nothing with me. It's got to end.
I peek through the door. You're digging my roots.

    You peek through my roots, start digging me up.
    No one's ever gotten this deep before.

No one's this deep. What's gotten into you?
You're filling holes I didn't know were there.

    I know my holes will be filled if you're there.
    I love the way you smile planting seeds.

The way you're planting me makes me smile
for my heart. Since you're near it we can grow.

You Satisfy Me

When you looked at me with love in your eyes
I thought you were playing tricks on my heart.

        I thought my heart was tricking me, playing
        with forces I didn't quite understand.

Yet, you didn't force me to understand
what I felt. You watered me all the same.

        You felt the same. I watered all of you.
        We grew beyond our imaginations.

We don't imagine why we grew beyond
reach. There's enough us to ease our hunger.

        We reached for our hunger enough. There's ease
        at our fingertips today. We're grateful.

I tip my fingers toward great full days
when you look at me with love in your eyes.

Holy Ascent

I wake up thinking of nothing but you,
your face glows brightly outside my window.

    My face is your window. Glowing inside
    are parts of me no one else bothers with.

I bother with one part of me. Are no
bodies stuck in my gravity? Maybe

    my gravity is stuck on your body.
    How is it that you've grown to hold my weight?

How is it that I've grown holding this weight?
I feel seen. I feel heard. I swallow life.

    You swallow what I feel. You've seen the life I
    give. I've lost my hungry will to what's left.

I will give what's left to us. I've lost most
ways to think. Nothing wakes me up but you.

I Hurt Us When I Left You Alone

We lived together in lavender fields
full of sheep and goats that graze all day long.

        All day long we grow berries and veggies,
        whisper to each other about right now.

Right now each whisper to each other fills
the well for days. We water everything.

        For days everything is well. We drink it.
        Then a bright falling star catches my eyes.

My eyes fall away from you like a star
could feed me how you do when we're touching.

        When I couldn't touch you I wasn't fed.
        I ate my heart since it's all I had left.

I ate my heart since I couldn't eat you
how I did when we still lived together.

Duplex (The My Heart Blues)

My heart is happy running in the grass
with nothing but the sunlight in its eyes.

    There's nothing left in the eyes of my heart
    except the light it hungers for at night.

At night it hungers for the light it sees –
doesn't ask permission before it eats.

    It doesn't ask permission when it feasts,
    just devours the patience I have left.

It devours the last of my patience
and burns the palms of those who hold it close.

    I can only trust those who hold it close.
    They know the truth of why we live apart.

They know the truth of why my heart won't start.
My heart is busy running in the grass.

I Was Damaged By My Disability

First I fail myself. Break my limbs. Give up.
I search for Lake Michigan. Eat fish raw.

    I eat Lake Michigan raw. Search for fish
    to talk to. They spit up popping bubbles.

They pop up to talk. I spit out bubbles
that float. I'm left unheard. Flying birds hear.

    Flying birds left. I float unheard words. Then
    I bury myself in the silent woods.

The silent woods have winding paths buried
out of sight. You walk by. I speak to you.

    We speak out of sight. You walk towards me.
    I drown in your light. My words burst open.

I drown in your words. You burst through my light.
You water me. My limbs heal. I get up.

I’m Just Happy You’re Here

You’re fire. It’s warm when you look my way.
I don’t want to share your stare. I’m selfish.

You’re selfish. You don’t want to see me shine.
We both devour the light in the room.

Light in the room can’t be shared by us both.
I don’t mind letting you have the first bite.

Mind, I always let you have the first bite
since we got together. What will I eat?

We will eat together since we got light.
A piece of you, a piece of me. We’re full.

We’re full of pieces. A piece starts to glow.
Who does this belong to? We both made it.

We made what doesn’t belong. It is us.
You’re warm. It's fire when you come my way.

You Taught Me My Heart Has A Face

I lie in the garden and speak to trees
about you. My heart won't leave them alone.

    You won't leave my heart alone. The trees bloom
    flowers by the time we meet at sunrise.

We meet by the flowers during sunrise.
The world is on fire all around us.

    The fire is us. Around the world all
    people wish they can burn without dying.

Without burning people wish they can die.
It pains me to live any other way.

    Another way to live is through the pain.
    The familiar sound of the setting sun.

Your familiar sound stops the sun setting
in the garden. We speak beneath the trees.

What Does My Heart Miss?

A bite of warm cheesecake from the oven.
Eating cake with milk chocolate frosting.

    Eating almonds covered in chocolate.
    My family watching television.

Television singing, family yapping,
barbeques with leftovers for a week.

    Having leftover barbeque for weeks
    gaming on a bean bag in the basement.

Lying on a bean bag in the basement
howling having sex with the one I love.

    Talking after sex with the one I love,
    tattooing their memory to my chest.

Tattooing my memories to my chest –
bites of warmth I can pull from the oven.

What I Want From You

I want to make you happy. I study
your smile. Research what you love. I'm on

    character watch. I'm on your smile like
    I'm getting payed. There's hugs, tea, and blankets.

I'm not paying for the tea and get hugs?
Forget living in the dark, you're sunshine!

    Forget sunshine, you make the world darker!
    Let's get lost. Let's build bridges. Let's climb high

to where bridges disappear. Let's get high
and watch anime. You and I shaking

    with laughter and tears. I watch you and shake
    stars from space. They orbit you. So many

stars, so much space. From orbit you're shining.
I study your happiness. I want to.

Wrapped In Nonsense

The dragon rises in the sky. We watch
in complete silence. We're struck by our fear.

We fear the silence where we're incomplete.
It's broken by our chatter about grass.

Our chattering is broken by the wind.
Though it's far away we feel heated breath.

This breath feels like the heat we tuck away
in empty parts of us. I'm warm but chill.

I'm empty. In parts of us I'm warm. Chill,
we're running out of food and I'm thirsty.

Out of food and full of thirst we run where
we can rest forever. There's room for one.

Forever we rest hugging with no room,
watch the sky. Smoke rises in the distance.

You

You tore apart my conceptions of light,
it's more than beauty, more than a strong voice.
All I know of light happens when one fights,
pick apart their glow so they have no choice.

You bring another kind of violence —
unapologetic love that shines close
to where the heart is. You are tireless,
ready to pounce on each person that shows.

But no one minds when being maimed by you,
the gentle touch from all your punches thrown
reminds people the love they feel is true,
each stranger wishes they can bring you home.

I'm in love with the fire in your eyes
a light so warm I'll always feel alive.

You Make Me Burst

Please,
say my name
again. Scream it
like black coffee.
I worship you
as weeds do
the sun. Like
bread and cheese.
I chew you until
my jaw is sore.
Our monsters play
Pantone while we
mix our colors.
We are new, but
you're familiar,
a ghost obsessing,
the big apple,
my right hook.
You got me through
and wanted more.
I give it to you
like my life depends
on keeping promises.
We make them
like knots enrich us.
We tie our ends
into floppy bows.
We do it again and
again and again.

II The Bad

The My Heart Blues

I don't know what I'm missing but I see
wind blowing that I can't quite grab onto
warms my heart then it falls to the street,
vanishes in silence, scared to be true.

I wade in waters too rough to swim in –
I'm moving so I don't mind the emptiness
grows in my chest. There a name for this sin?
I poke and prod and understand it less.

Why can't I grow past memories of when?
When I didn't care what ignorance was.
Did I forget to ignore life again?
I think of it so much I turn to dust.

Parts of me wonder how vast my heart is,
parts of me wish I could live without this.

my heart needs to pull its own weight

my heart stops chasing after the wind
my heart grows bored staring at clouds
my heart is no longer impressed by trees
my heart starts wandering the neighborhood
my heart doesn't get along with any neighbors
my heart cries about it in our room at night
my heart picks up skateboarding in the park
my heart watches fish swim in the river
my heart makes friends with the soccer players
my heart sticks to playing defense
my heart gets home tired every evening
my heart tracks mud into the living room
my heart leaves before doing the dishes
my heart hits me when I ask it to clean its mess
my heart and I have a talk about communication
my heart won't apologize to me
my heart comes home later and later
my heart stops talking to me altogether
my heart returns sad one day
my heart has hurt another person
my heart is no longer welcome at the park
my heart starts wandering downtown
my heart is kickin it with these cool dudes
my heart won't let anyone else in the room talk
my heart gets mad when people start to leave
my heart does a handstand for attention
my heart is ashamed at how far it will go
my heart moves alone to the woods

my heart swings a stick at the sun
my heart takes years to forget the shame
my heart comes home with a blade of grass
my heart apologizes for its past behavior
my heart promises to be more patient for us
my heart decides to grow a garden
my heart plants sprouts that glow at night

What Lives Between Us

I can’t reach you
across this ocean.
My reflection stares
at my failure.
I return home alone.
It feels empty
with you outside
the kitchen window.
I dig up my roots
to meet you but
pieces of me die.
I accept the holes,
they remind me of you.
For years the gap
doesn’t close.
You’re further
away. I draw maps
of what’s born
from your debris.
New moons
orbit your head.
Satellites, meteors,
and dead suns can’t
escape your gravity.
I want your heavenly body
but I won't survive
the flight. I'm left
insecure. I shoot

sounding rockets
to make sense
of your atmosphere.
The data is beyond
my grasp. My fingers
snap trying to hold it.
I'm left with no choice
but to let go.

You Ate Me Up

You're not gentle when you bite into me.
Moms the only one to hit me this hard.

    This is hard for mom. She doesn't like you,
    says there's no way you can take care of me.

You don't even try to take care of me,
it's not who you are. You're busy eating.

    You're busy eating who I am, a meal
    you don't need to cook. I'm cocked and ready.

I'm ready to cook, you don't need to rush.
Please, give me some time to dress myself up.

    Sometimes I give myself up to please you.
    You're so deep in me I'm choking on blood.

You're so deep in blood and choking on me.
You're not gentle when you bite into me.

Bonded

When we met we were focused on growing.
We can't tell you that we lived a good life.

Our good life can't tell you that we lived well.
It's a small amount of things we got right.

We're right about small things. It's a big deal.
I lose myself in failure. My pool's deep.

I lose in my deep pool like a failure.
I'm a better runner than a swimmer.

I'm running to get better. I swim down.
I see us even when I'm blind. We're soft.

I'm lost. I'm blind even when we're both seen.
I don't have good reasons for us to stay.

One good reason for us to stay is we're
growing, that we've been focused since we met.

I Don't Know How To Speak To My Father

What do I say to the ghost in my room?
I stare at him silently mouthing words.

    I stare words into him silently and
    wish they wouldn't sink through translucent skin.

I wish it wasn't translucent. His skin
must be ice cold to the touch. His heart dead.

    Must be cold to be dead. My heart is touched
    by this haunt. Did he pick me or the room?

Maybe he haunts this room and picks nothing.
I didn't get to choose. I just accept.

    I just accept the ghost didn't choose me.
    I'm done divining what that means for us.

I divine what it means to live with ghosts.
What else can I do? He stays in my room.

I Know You Don't Care About Me

My heart tried to tell me for years. Listen!
Why can't I just take it seriously?

        Seriously, why? I can't just take it
        for granted. I figure it knows better.

Granted, you are better. It's figured out
I spent another day thinking of you.

        I think of another day I won't spend
        all my time fighting my heart. I must stop.

I stop fighting all the time. My heart cries,
that's not what it meant. I misunderstood.

        I don't understand what it meant. That's fucked.
        If I could give it what it wants I would.

Could it give me what I want? It would, right?
My heart listened to me for years. It tried.

I Only Know How To Love Your Body

My heart sobs in a tree under the sun.
It waits for you to send out a signal,

It waits for signals it can't interpret
since your body speaks its own language.

Your body speaks. A new language blooms
flowers my heart can't name. I want them plucked.

I can't ask you the flower's name. I pluck.
You wince from pain. What have we done, again?

We've done what we want, caused pain once again.
I boiled your blood by just listening.

My blood boils listening to you. Now,
I thirst for your body. My own hungers

for your thirst. I hunger for one more bite.
My heart sobs in a tree under the moon.

my blood has gone away

you and i
will never be
since my blood
gave up on me,
too. you both
share special
memories of
breathing heavy
under blankets.
of lavender coffee.
of fire. i boiled
my blood fighting
against the wind,
did it grow bored
of conquest?
my weapons can't
pour my blood
back into me —
my body is full
of what i miss.
i can only muster
courage to see
you and my blood enjoying
days in peace
beneath those trees
beside the lake
where you smell flowers
and gossip. love

needs no stoking,
so why did i try
to breathe it to life?
i could never be
you and i –
maybe that is why
my blood won't
come home.

My Heart Doesn't Know How to Love Me

My heart has a grasp on my tongue and won't let go of my breath; holds me still in its arteries; tightens the walls around us; places me in the meadow. I become grass; the wind blows me away - I am free. My heart becomes jealous of the dirt I land on, now I have a mouthful of what I can't say because I'm afraid my heart is going to catch up to me, so I run up the creek. My heart is waiting for me when I get there and opens the door to the den. I take off my coat, my shoes, my skin, my muscles. My heart jumps into my chest. My heart speaks for the first time. My eyes well, my heart leaves to travel the world giving speeches. My heart returns home for the holiday. I have a family now. I tell my heart and it bursts into pieces. We hold a funeral for my heart, bury it in the backyard with everything we love. My heart grows into a tree overnight, bears one fruit that looks like my heart. My family cries at the beauty. I tremble. My heart beats back to life. My heart crawls down from the tree. I let my heart into my chest. My family is horrified to see my heart has come back to me.

My Heart Has Come Home

My heart has noticed what you think of us.
After it searched for ways to bring you back
it returned from the long trip on the bus
and cried to me about its complete lack

of insight. I listen to my heart whine.
It speaks its truth and its face lights up.
Without you it no longer sits and pines,
it seeks fresh ways to fill its empty cup.

What gift can I give to my broken heart?
Let us plant seeds to grow our own garden,
daily reasons to never again part.
We will celebrate the work we have done.

The truth is I don't miss you at night,
missed talking to my heart without a fight.

Moving Away From You

I wake up to you every morning.
It tastes like sunlight. Warm and fuzzy bites.

        It bites like it tastes. Fuzzy boundaries
        burn holes into my skin. I give them names.

Names I give burn into skin. My my my.
Who will I say goodnight to after this?

        After you're gone will I have a good night?
        There will be no one there to make me vanish.

No one will vanish with me there. Make me
truthful. Tell it how it is. I listen.

        Listen to how truthful this is. I tell
        the future now based on what's missing.

Now the future is based. Nothing missing.
I wake up for me every morning.

The Relationship Blues

I learned from mama, to keep my heart home.
Mama always told me, keep your heart home.
Who's gonna love you out there on your own?

Found friends who hug me, take me out sometimes.
Friends became homies, we partied sometimes.
My heart's so lonely, met no friends of mine.

My heart's in the garden, won't greet our guests.
My heart won't leave the bathroom, our guests left.
Now everyone's departed, my heart can rest.

Found me a lover, wants to meet my heart.
I brought home a lover, to meet my heart.
My heart didn't love her, our love fell apart.

My heart loves wasting time under blue skies,
nothing we can do to widen its eyes.

my heart needs to pull its own weight II

my heart names the sprouts after old friends
my heart watches them grow into saplings
my heart trims their leaves with its sword
my heart brings me to the garden to share its work
my heart opens up to me for the first time
my heart teaches me how to swing a sword
my heart falls in love with our training
my heart stops watering the plants
my heart can't get them to stop singing
my heart hears complaints from the neighbors
my heart decides to ask me for help
my heart doesn't understand why I say no
my heart leaves me with the garden
my heart watches me trim the trees with my sword
my heart critiques my swordplay
my heart won't listen when I ask it to leave
my heart says it wants to spend time with me
my heart doesn't know how to have a good time
my heart doesn't like the sound of that
my heart and I cross blades for a week straight
my heart loses when my slice slips past its parry
my heart laughs and tries to shake it off
my heart wonders why we're fighting
my heart and I decide to share the garden
my heart and I begin training together again
my heart and I are reminded of old times
my heart and I walk through the park together
my heart has turned over a new leaf

my heart glows red as it passionately speaks its mind
my heart doesn't know what to do with this feeling
my heart understands what it wants now
my heart tells me the truth
my heart and I are moved to tears
my heart has never been so open with me
my heart asks if we can spar together
my heart only speaks one language
my heart defeats me in three sword moves
my heart is finally starting to make some sense

I Know You Don't Care About My Heart

What am I supposed to tell it at night?
I'm the one who said to give you a try.

I'm not one to try. I give you my all.
My heart doesn't like when you won't hold it.

It doesn't like you. Holds its breath when you
play too much. I like that. Too bad it hurts.

I like that it hurts. Too bad I can't play.
I guess my heart thinks I've got a screw loose.

Screw my heart I guess. I've got to get loose
to have even a second of your time.

My time is second to yours. I have to
be honest with myself. My heart needs it.

It needs to be honest. Myself, too. I
suppose I'll tell it what I am tonight.

Even Though We Are Over

My heart would do most anything for you -
It sits in your shade to water your roots,

  It sits in your shade, forgets what it knows.
  I try to grow to bring my heart back home,

I try to grow without it back at home
since it only feels alive when you're new.

  My heart feels alive when your leaves are new.
  It names each flower and fruit that you grow,

it measures each branch and root that you grow.
Why won't it come have a look at me, too?

  Why won't it come try to water me, too?
  I won't grow while my heart's away working.

You'll grow while it's away. This won't work.
My heart is giving everything to you.

Love Changed My Heart

All day you live rent free in my big head.
I miss old thoughts of sword and fist fights –
simpler times when I won to get ahead.
Now, I wonder if I'm living life right.

What happened to the things I want to do?
Can I replace these thoughts with real action?
I've no desire to find a new crew
I've lost attachment to any faction.

Why'd I lose myself when I fell in love?
I've not lost so much of myself before.
I search for new hobbies that will help give
me dirt to grow on. I want nothing more.

This makes me never want to love again.
I hope I can grow past the me from then.

Lost Without the Light

Looking in her eyes I feel a dire fire.
I would never leave her, I desire fire.

Without her heat I forget how to breathe.
Why did she have to hide her fire?

With her gone no one shines light on me,
I'm waiting for the sun to inspire fire.

These ashes do not come with instructions
on revitalization. I wish I could just hire fire.

Morning never comes so I seek new light
to remind me of the warmth of a prior fire.

To find my own light I plant seeds in the dirt,
one day they will grow tall enough to acquire fire

without the sun. My sprouts fail to grow an inch —
deep in the dirt I learn they require fire

to grow into saplings. I must tend to their glowing
by shining bright myself. How could I learn to perspire fire?

I set out to the woods where the tallest trees grow
to become someone who seeks higher fire.

In the dark woods I build a camp under the moon
staring at the coals I wonder, why her fire?

In the canopies I reach into the sky with a fist,
from these heights I feel the depths of my entire fire.

I Lament it took so long to find my heart burning.
I often think of her when I admire fire.

How Many Years Have I Been Gone?

After two years we stop using our names.
Why complicate our closeness with old words?

    Old closeness complicates our words. New ones
    shape us into unique animals. Damn.

We're animals with unique shapes. We're damned.
Who will recognize what we've become now?

    We will. What becomes of who we've been?
    That's for our parents to worry about.

About our parents, they worry for years
since we looked away from our family.

    Why did I look away from family?
    Seven years in I can't remember why.

Seven years in I can't remember me.
After eight years we start using our names.

III The Dark

Duplex (I Can't Begin With Love)

Could be my heart never belonged to me
since I was fighting before I could weep,

since I was fighting before I could scream,
I learned a language no one else could speak.

I didn't learn a language I could speak
to tell my momma what she means to me.

To tell my father what he means to me
I beat up every boy that made me feel –

I brought home every girl that made me feel
my heart has found the only light it needs.

My heart has never found the light it needs
to feed the garden thriving inside me.

The garden feeds. Vines, roots, bulbs, swallow me!
Could be my heart will never get to breathe.

Duplex (I Can't Begin With Me)

Could be my heart will never get to breathe.
It stokes my fire down on bloody knees.

> My bloody fire dims down stoking me
> to grow my life into a golden tree.

My life will grow into a golden tree
when nature's light blows wind into me —

> I bury nature's light into my chest
> to find the meaning hiding in the leaves.

I found the meaning hiding in the leaves
when I embraced the sun that's in between.

> When I embraced the sun I couldn't see
> the shadows filling up the cracks in me.

The shadows fill me. Who am I to be?
Could be my heart is all that's left of me.

Duplex (I Can't Begin With My Heart)

Could be my heart is all that's left of me.
I built a home inside the raging sea –

the home inside the sea is built empty.
The wind gives me the company I need,

the company gives me the wind I need,
I listen to the embers deep in me.

The embers listen to me speak deeply
of brighter stars than where we rest our feet.

I was a brighter star than the rest of folks
but then my heart began to burden me.

My heart began to burden how I grew
above the clouds where I could find some peace.

Above the clouds I find some peace in dreams.
Could be my heart just wants me to be free.

Duplex (I Can't Begin With Her)

Could be my heart just wants me to be free
from all the times she had her way with me,

    from all the times she didn't let me be,
    I changed into a person without teeth.

I failed into a change without trying
and I can't stop the falling of my leaves;

    My leaves stop falling and I am drying
    because her fire hides the light from me.

Because her fire hides light from the sun
my heart has never wondered what will come.

    My heart has never wondered how to be
    just grew to heights I couldn't love to see.

Our love just grew to heights I couldn't see.
Could be my heart has loved her more than me.

Duplex (I Can't Begin With Needs)

Could be my heart has loved her more than me.
She brings my heart stargazing on the lake,

    she brings my heart to picnics on the beach
    so they both smile happy as can be.

They smile happy living without me
because I never gave them anything –

    because I never gave up being me
    I lost sight of the light my heart could eat,

I lost sight of the light to feed my heart
to make me who it is I'm meant to be.

    To become who it is I'm meant to be
    I pray my heart one day returns to me.

I pray to grow so tall my heart can see.
Could be my heart has everything it needs.

Duplex (I Can't Begin With Talk)

Could be my heart has everything it needs,
a silent cry that echoes in my chest.

    My echoes cry in that chest. A silent
    plea won't be able to fill the empty.

The empty plea is able to fill me
since we keep growing when we are apart.

    Since we keep growing when we are apart
    I show it memories etched in my bark.

I shed the memories etched in my bark
the day I come to listen to my heart.

    I come to listen to my heart complain
    and now I cannot hide from what it wants.

From now on it cannot hide what it wants,
could be my heart can only see the sun.

Duplex (I Can't Begin With Fire)

Could be my heart can only see the sun.
It gives up on the few leaves that I've grown.

    I must give up the few leaves that I've grown
    so we can become what we've never known.

We've never known what we can become, an
emptiness that chews on me like a beast.

    That emptiness chews me then I'm a beast –
    I fill it with any light I can drink,

I drink to fill it with what light I can –
my heart won't eat a shred of what I bring,

    you won't find a shred of what brings my heart.
    I worry it's as hungry as I am.

I worry that it's as done as I am.
It has always watched me fail to be.

    It has always failed to watch me through.
    Could be my heart has learned what it can do.

Duplex (I Can't Begin With My Mother)

Could be my heart has learned what it can do
when it healed from being used by you.

It's healed from being used every day
after I burned my memories of you.

Mother, why did I burn our memories?
I have been an unfilial child,

I haven't called you for a long while –
I'm afraid to walk into your good mood,

I'm afraid to dance to your pushy tune.
You think the stars are shining just for you.

Since you think stars are shining just for you
you'll never understand why you're alone,

you'll never know why I don't visit home.
Could be my heart is sad it can't love you.

Duplex (I Can't Begin With My Twin)

Could be my heart is sad it can't love you
since we fought over a plate of cold fries.

We fought over a bed with no mattress
to see who got to sleep on the carpet.

To see who got to wear new shoes
I studied hard to be who mother chose,

I studied hard to be away from home
to let my heart prance free beneath the moon.

My heart pranced free beside the shallow lake
fishing without breath how father taught us.

Father taught us how to hide our breath
when we leave behind the trees we grow.

Now, I will leave behind the tree we grew.
Could be my heart wants nothing else from you.

Duplex (I Can't Begin With My Father)

Could be my heart wants nothing else from you.
You pick apart it's green glowing garden,

    you pick apart it's sporty wrinkled clothes –
    you can't fathom the work that keeps it full,

you can't fathom the full that it works for,
why would I toast beers at your barbeque?

    Why should I ever pour one out for you?
    I learned love from that nigga down the street,

I learned to love each nigga that I meet
and it doesn't help me understand you,

    and it doesn't help me to forget you
    since I see your face when I hear my name.

Since I faced that all we share is your name
could be my heart is done fighting for you.

Duplex (I Can’t Begin With Friends)

Could be my heart is done fighting for you
to notice how I’m drooling for your light.

        It watches how I’m drooling for your light
        then plants lavender where you rest your head.

It plants lavender with berries that glow –
you water them like they belong to you.

        You water them like my heart is your own
        but I’ve made plans to dig you from your roots,

but I’ve made plans to dig my hands in you
so let's feast on what has blossomed between us.

        Between us the blossoms feast on what is.
        With juice on our faces we grow apart.

My heart’s full with juice so we grow apart.
Could be my heart is sick with light from you.

Duplex (I Can't Begin With Relationships)

Could be my heart is sick with light from you.
We watch my fire. We laugh, joke, and play.

We laugh, joke, and play. My fire goes out.
I'd rather shine but I storm through the house.

I'd rather shine but I'm a lightning storm
prying each locked door open with worn hands.

I pry each window open with worn hands –
I shout at the sea to warn you I would.

I shout at cracked walls to warn you I could
since we both understand a broken home.

I broke when I couldn't understand home
can be peaceful as fields of lavender.

I'm not at peace in fields of lavender –
could be my heart burns way too hot for you.

Duplex (I Can't Begin With Us)

Could be my heart burns way too hot for you,
you call them jokes but the words sting my heart.

The words sting my heart, you call me a punk –
I punch my pillow then I wipe my tears.

I punch the window then I wipe my blood
as if nothing good happened between us,

as if nothing good happened I move on –
alone with my heart as it croons at night.

I listen to it croon alone at night
and worry about how it misses you.

I worry about what it's been missing
since I only make history repeat.

Since I only repeat our history
could be my heart is getting bored of me.

Duplex (I Begin With Light)

Could be my heart is getting bored of me
hunting inside your shadow for the light.

    I hunt inside your shadow for the light
    to eat what no one wants. There's no fighting.

I eat what no one wants since there's no fight –
it's important to me, like drinking sun.

    I drink the sun. It's important to be
    brighter. Without it night will swallow me.

Night swallows without me. My will's brighter.
I show up to shoot lightning from my eyes.

    I show up to shoot my light just for you
    though I'm stuck here shining without my heart.

Since I'm stuck here shining without my heart
could be my heart never belonged to me.

IV The Ugly

The My Heart Blues

My heart wipes the sweat from its brow,
the sprouts are growing well. The sun beams
down on them, but they are brighter.
My heart has been waiting for this day,
finally, a use for the sprouts –
our problems evaporate in their warmth,
or so it tells me. We speak
about it over dinner, my heart weary
from working outside. I ask
about the weather, it mumbles
about fireflies sucking nectar
from the sprout's leaves. It tells me
tomorrow there will be nothing left
to keep us here. I thank it for its growth.
Apart from me it has no one to tend
the garden so I tell it tomorrow
I will come dressed in overalls with a bucket
filled with fertilizer. My heart sighs.
It slams the door on its way back outside
without me. I open the window
to watch it pull the last sprout
from the dirt. It's time to find new soil.
This place is overrun with what we can't solve.
I tell my heart not to worry,
we'll grow sprouts so strong
nothing will be born from their shadows.
They'll shine so brightly.
It asks me how I know.
I can't tell it the truth,
I brought this darkness home.

Because of My Love You Always Have Something To Take From Me

First you took my time. I gave it away.
It was something that we both could enjoy.

    Was that we both enjoy something could be.
    Second to go was my vision. Can't see.

My vision was to see seconds go by.
Lost my voice right after. Speak slower please,

    speak after please, use the right voice. I'm lost.
    Then dreams. Without them I hate sleep. That, too.

Without that then I hate dreams. Who am I?
Someone who can't even get up for work.

    I can't even get worked up for someone
    who shows me the best version of themselves.

I showed you the best version of myself.
You took it away. I still gave my time.

How To Fail Them

Eat them. Forget to chew. Choke. Throw them up.
Save you a piece. Put the rest in the fridge.

Put the piece of them to rest. Save the day.
Write them letters. Ask what they think about.

Think about letters they would write you back.
Wonder why you ate them. Realize pain.

Wonder why pain ate you. Realize light.
Feel the burn. Wade into the lake at night.

Burn the lake into your eyes. Feel the night
recoil from the soft touch of seaweed.

Recoil from the soft touch of your fear.
Hurry home. Bury them in the backyard.

Bury them a yard down. Hurry back. Cry.
Forget how to eat. Choke on tears. Miss them.

I Trust My Heart is Watering Plants

As it climbs out of my chest I lie
and say I can fix the cracks growing
in its veins. There's a way to be free
of the danger, in a meadow of our own
I plant sprouts that glow like the sun
but it's not what my heart wants.
My heart only knows how to run
so it leaves searching for you.
I have no choice but to play along
if I want my heart to come home.
You left because my heart won't tend
to the seeds it plants. If it knew the truth
it would perish. I grow this garden
to watch fresh blooms, for us to be free
of you. My heart values freedom
less and less, just wants to blaze
with you in the moonlight.
I miss you as much as my heart
but you never once planted seeds
in this place I had made for us –
there's none of your light left.
Will my heart starve?
I water my sprouts to find
what is left of me. I count petals
to forget your name, but I'll never forget
how you filled us to the brim with laughter,
broke our ties to the dirt, left my heart
wandering across steep mountaintops.

I would come to miss our garden
though my heart was thrilled to be
miles away from where we till soil.
My heart has forgotten what matters,
all the more reason for you to go
search for one that knows.

I’m Afraid Of My Schizophrenia

I’m afraid of losing light. I get it,
I’ve changed colors since yesterday. I’m new.
I’m afraid you’ll have to relearn to fit
in with me. It’s my voice with a fresh view.

Am I uncanny? Like a flesh robot
reciting memories? They’re all I have
left of me. Can we start again? I thought
doctors could help. My still fractured brain veers

into today ramming against my loves.
I hope those won’t change. I’m afraid they will
when I reset, when I’m bid from above
to let go, when this light ends. I can’t chill.

I’m afraid there is no answer. Problems
will arise. I’m afraid we won't blossom.

Young Love

She looks at the world like it's an old friend.
Who wouldn't want a taste of that hot shit?

    Shit she's hot. I would want a taste of who
    can't stand her. They must know something I don't.

Something I don't know can't be right. Must be her.
This why I'm listening to all she says?

    I'm listening with all my heart. This burns.
    I need to drink her wiles now! Fuck life.

Fuck her. Now her wiles drink what I need.
There's no room for me in her car's backseat.

    Back in her room there's a lonely seat
    I'm stuck in. Mom told me I should leave her.

Mom, I'm stuck. Should I leave? I told myself
she'll look at my face when I'm an old friend.

Mother Gave Me Everything She Never Gave Weather

She leaves. The wind breathes a sigh of relief.
Weather isn't on her side and knows it.

Weather knows her side isn't rain or shine.
She only loves the sky when it's bright.

She only loves when the sky will listen.
It's too bad she won't let clouds be themselves.

She says clouds are too bad. They lose themselves,
cry for days, and scream back. She hates the sounds.

She screams back with hate. Animals cry sounds.
She feels bad for the innocent young ones.

They're ignorant. She feels their kindness
and smiles. It's real, then they grow up fast.

They grow real. There's no more smiles. They leave.
Weather can't leave her. She sighs with relief.

My Blood Is Trying To Kill Me

My blood will boil from anyone's touch.
I don't like people near me. My heart knows.

People I like near me don't know my heart
since my blood gets in the way of talking.

I can't talk when my blood catches fire.
It burns holes into my heart no one sees.

The holes burn my eyes. My heart sees. What now?
I can't stop my blood rushing out fist first.

I throw the first punch. There's blood on my fist.
My heart is glad that it's not the victim.

I'm the victim. My heart gets in the way
of our fighting. It beats hard and can't breathe.

My heart is dying. I'm fighting to breathe.
Anyone's touch will save us from my blood.

When I Let Go Of You I Fell Apart

I learned love from a wrecking ball. It hurts
to be struck by the truth. Did I forget
how simple our love is? We didn't flirt
once. We watch each other grow tall and sweat

our clothes off in comfort. It's not awkward
revealing my secrets. Well, not to you.
I want the world to see this way forward –
kimbap, crocheted yarn, fire. It's taboo

for love to be painless. Where's the power
in giving? There's none, only freedom
from worship, obsession, and the soured
taste of want. Without it I fail to see

I lost the sun. I can't seem to recall
when life turned me into a wrecking ball.

My Love Isn't Over Yet

It's time that I accept that you have left.
I'm living with this fire in my chest.

With fire living in me there's no rest –
I burn to ashes like a cigarette.

The cigarettes burn my clothes to ashes.
The world can see it like a powdered nose.

The world can see it like the powdered snow
falling where the sunlight will never go.

The sun will go where falling light never
creates the world that makes you understand.

I understand the world that you create.
You lit me up, it rewired my brain.

You rewired me, lit me through the dark.
It's time that I accept you have my heart.

I Keep Failing You

Whoa! You never ask me for anything.
I don't know what it is I do for you.

What I do know is I do it for you.
My efforts evaporate like water.

My efforts drown your voice out like water.
I hear the sound of being left behind.

Behind the sound I can hear your being.
We did everything to keep you full.

After everything we did, I keep full.
Where our love had grown is now a black hole.

Where's our love? Now that a black hole has grown
I only continue to feed it me

and it continues only to feed me.
You never asked me for this empty thing.

You Speak To Me Like We're Enemies

Short. Not sweet. Missing the point. In bad faith.
Make up what I did cuz of what you felt.

Cuz you felt one can't make up what I did
it's over. Guns out. Take no prisoners.

Its guns, and tongues take over when they're out.
No more making sense of what's a bother.

No bothering to make sense of conflict.
Momma taught you right with a back hand fist.

Momma taught you talk back and her right fist
answers hard questions you don't even have.

You don't question how hard you have to brace,
only come calm, collected, and prepared.

Prepared to come collect only calm love.
Short and sweet. Not missing. In good faith.

With You I'm Never Certain Of My Place

Is today going to be a good day?
Am I to blame or do I solve problems?

    Am I a problem or do I blame love
    for the smile on my face? I'm happy

when you smile. I'm facing your happy
times like the well will dry any day now.

    Will times like now dry my days out or will
    I hold your body to the sun to grow.

You grow in the sun and hide my body.
I haven't moved an inch. I'm animal.

    I haven't moved an inch. I'm animal.
    How could I have made a mistake shitting?

Could I mistake what I have made for mine?
Am I going to lose my say today?

I'm Full Of Your Love For Me

This is one thing that we have in common.
Another is violence against me.

> Against violence another me is there.
> You like looking at the face I don't know.

Don't you like the face I know? Look at me!
I starve though I'm full of our history.

> Since my history is full of starving
> I find home in warm places that burn me.

You're warm. I burn my home to find your place.
I only know how to start from nothing.

> I know nothing from the start, only feel
> the clouds parting and the sun shining bright.

Shining clouds brighten the sky. The sun dips.
This common thing is all that you left me.

My Father Never Cared About My Heart

My brothers and I take turns playing games,
one hour at a time between us four.

        The four of us spent hours at a time
        sat at home unable to use the stove.

We're unable to use the fridge. We sat
hungry, ate dry cereal for lunch.

        At dinner we're hungry. Fuck dry cereal.
        I wanted to cook myself a pork steak.

Stepmother won't let me cook for myself,
she's bad at it. Made thick raw hamburgers.

        Raw burgers taste bad. My vomit is thick.
        I'm in the basement with my sleeping bag.

In my sleeping bag on the basement floor
my step brothers take turns playing a game.

My Heart Doesn't Slash the Same Around You

I've lost control of my life
since my heart just wants to run
from the danger of being open.
The sun bares down on my skin,
warms the emptiness in me –
my heart sips coffee and chats
about freedom from the heat.
It misses those nights
when the moon would glow
we swung our swords wildly
with leaves falling around us.
It is fond of the dance,
wants to grow stronger veins
to protect me from you. It cuts
deep into the night – slashes
honed with purpose and intent
to never let you have your way.
I am fond of watching it
carry out the only conviction
it shows. Now I know it
will never let us grow closer.
Why has my heart become stubborn?
What else will we lose to you
since we can't control the way
you make us feel? My heart
wants to leave you behind, but I never
want to spend another day without you.
It will never find peace

since it wants things to never change.
Does it know that means it will stay
the same, unable to make its dreams
come true? A world without you.

I Was Always Bright Fire Before I Met You

You never helped me come to see my worth.
I fed you then you grew larger than earth.

Rather than grow larger I fed you earth
that seeps its way into our living room.

The living seeps it's way into my room –
screaming, blaming, and vengeful attitudes.

Blaming vengeful screams on an attitude
resolves you of the damage you can do.

Can the damage resolve with you still loose?
Bless dinnertime where we can laugh and goof.

We laugh where we are blessed by goofy truths
until you are annoyed my fire blew.

You blow my fire annoyed that it's cool
so you never come to see my burning.

I Can't Think Clearly When You Look At Me

It feels like I have reached the end of life.
I shouldn't have to make you tell me twice.

> I shouldn't have to make you hold the knife.
> How do I attract this angry fighting?

How do angry fights attract this heat
that numbs my legs and pains my heart to beat?

> I beat my legs and pain my heart to go
> and sink beneath the lake where it can sleep.

To sleep where it can sink beneath your gaze
I smile with my eyes and grit my teeth.

> I smile with my eyes to keep my teeth
> so sadness doesn't take my time away.

The time sadness doesn't take me away
I'll feel like I have reached the end of days.

When I Think of Her

I count the tiles on the kitchen floor,
ripples in the ceiling, drips in the sink,

    ripples in the sink. The ceiling drips
    silence. Without her it's loud. My breath hides.

The silence hides her. I hear my loud breath.
For one, I cooked for us out of habit.

    I cooked for us for seven years. For one,
    I forget I'm alone. For two, I waste

food. I forget I'm no longer two. Waste
time watering the sun, eating starlight.

    I drink sunlight then starve eating water,
    again. I learn just how simple I am.

Again, I learn that I am so simple
I count the tiles on the kitchen floor.

Author Bio

Lamont Arrington is a writer from Grand Rapids, Michigan. He completed undergraduate studies at Grand Valley State University in 2017 and graduate studies at Central Michigan University in 2025, both in Creative Writing with an emphasis on Poetry. In 2018 he won the Dyer Ives award for his poem, "Niggas in Paradise." His first full length poetry collection, "Classless" was published in 2022. "The My Heart Blues" is his second full length collection published in 2026. Lamont currently works as an adjunct professor at Grand Rapids Community College and spends his days focused on writing. Social media @AiryArri

www.ingramcontent.com/pod-product-compliance
Lightning Source LLC
Chambersburg PA
CBHW071354230926
51846CB00002B/556
9781968226091